LIVING PROCESSES

Animal Variation and Classification

Richard Spilsbury

rosen publishing's
rosen central

New York

Published in 2010 by The Rosen Publishing Group Inc.
29 East 21st Street, New York, NY 10010

Editors: Sarah Eason and Leon Gray
Editor for Wayland: Julia Adams
Designer: Paul Myerscough
Illustrator: Geoff Ward
Picture researcher: Maria Joannou
Consultant: Michael Scott OBE

First Edition

Library of Congress Cataloging-in-Publication Data

Spilsbury, Richard, 1963-
Animal variation and classification / Richard Spilsbury. -- 1st ed.
    p. cm. -- (Living processes)
Includes index.
ISBN 978-1-61532-344-9 (library binding)
ISBN 978-1-61532-347-0 (paperback)
ISBN 978-1-61532-357-9 (6-pack)
1. Animals--Classification--Juvenile literature. 2. Animals--
Variation--Juvenile literature. I. Title.
QL352.S65 2010
590.1'2--dc22

                    2009030564

Photo Credits:
Fotolia: Penny 41t, Ribe 27; Shutterstock: Victoria Alexandrova 30, John A. Anderson 26b, Konovalikov Andrey
31, Yuri Arcurs 10, Asasirov 33t, Stephen Bonk 35t, P Borowka 23, Alex James Bramwell 37c, Troy Casswell
24, ClimberJAK 13t, Dusty Cline 20, Matthew Cole 19b, Dakotaboy 14, Jan Daly 15b, Kristof Degreef 3, 41b,
Craig Dingle 29b, Dennis Donohue 12, EcoPrint 36, 38, Fivespots 17, Susan Flashman 37t, Four Oaks 19cl,
Goldenangel 22, Ilya D. Gridnev 6, Lavigne Herve 21, Eric Isselée 13br, 19t, Rey Kamensky 35b, Sebastian
Kaulitzki 16, Bartlomiej K. Kwieciszewski 32, Linda Macpherson 7, Joze Maucec 25t, Christian Musat 39t,
Andrei Nekrassov 33b, Shawn Pecor 11l, Nikolai Pozdeev 13bl, Psamtik 4, 15t, Hiroyuki Saita 5, 37b, Stefan
Schejok 9, 19cr, Elisei Shafer 25b, Asther Lau Choon Siew 26t, Audrey Snider-Bell 28, Snowleopard1 34,
Nikita Tiunov 29, Shane White 40, Tracy Whiteside 11r.
Cover: Shutterstock/Susan Flashman.

Manufactured in China
CPSIA Compliance Information: Batch #WAW0102YA: For Further Information contact Rosen Publishing, New York, New York at 1-800-237-9932

SAFETY NOTE: The activities in this book are intended for children.
However, we recommend adult supervision at all times since neither the
Publisher nor the author can be held responsible for any injury.

Contents

CHAPTER 1

Introducing classification

The natural world is made up of an enormous variety of living things, from algae, alligators, and anteaters to ferns, frogs, and fungi. In fact, there are millions of different life forms, or species, in the world. Millions more have yet to be discovered.

Sorting species

Scientists use classification to identify and sort these species into groups based on similarities in the way they look or behave. This helps them make sense of nature and understand the relationships between different species.

Origins of classification

It is human nature to try to organize things into groups—the natural world is no exception. Just as librarians classify books so that people can find all the biology books on one shelf and all the novels by one author on another, scientists group similar species to make their lives easier.

The first people to classify were probably trying to tell the edible and useful organisms apart from the harmful ones. They organized things based on the way they looked and whether people had been poisoned by them.

Takifugu bimaculatus is the Latin name for the Japanese pufferfish. The fish is eaten as a delicacy in Japan, where it is commonly known as *fugu*, which means "river pig."

One of the first attempts of a scientific classification was made by a philosopher from ancient Greece named Aristotle (384–322 BCE).

Aristotle grouped living things not just by the way they looked, but also by the way they behaved and how their bodies were arranged.

Over time, classification became more accurate. Developments in technology were vital—such as microscopes to study the tiny world of cells. So, too, was the cooperation between the scientists who devoted their careers to compare and confirm classifications. Today, scientists can tell very similar organisms apart by comparing information such as cell structure, the genetic makeup inside cells, and other fine details. These advances are constantly pushing scientists to question and revise how they classify species.

WHAT'S IN A NAME?

Classification started to get confused when scientists used different names for the same organism. For example, an elk in North America is known as a red deer in Europe. To prevent this type of confusion, the Swedish scientist Carolus Linnaeus (1707–1778) came up with a new way of naming species. He gave everything two names. The first is the genus name—similar to your last or family name. The second is the species name—similar to your first name. This so-called Latin name is now used by every scientist in the world. One species may have several common names, but only one Latin name. The Latin name for the North American elk and European red deer is *Cervus elaphus*.

This European red deer is classified by its Latin name, *Cervus elaphus*.

What is an animal?

An enormous variety of animals live on our planet. Different animals make their homes in every habitat on Earth, from the frozen polar regions to the murky ocean depths. Despite their different shapes and sizes, all animals share certain basic features. Animal bodies are made up of cells, which usually group together to form tissues and organs. Animal cells are surrounded by a cell membrane, which encloses tiny structures called organelles. The nucleus is an organelle. It contains deoxyribonucleic acid (DNA), which contains the instructions that allow organisms to live their lives.

DNA determines how every animal looks and how it functions.

All about food

Unlike plant cells, animal cells do not have rigid cell walls or organelles called chloroplasts. In plant cells, chloroplasts make food for the plant using the energy of the sun. This process is called photosynthesis. Animals cannot make their own food, so they have to eat plants or other animals.

Most animals have a central nervous system to sense their surroundings and a digestive system to absorb the energy in their food. Most animals also need to move—either to find food or to avoid being eaten.

Sheep must feed on plants, such as grass, to take in energy to perform everyday functions, such as breathing and moving.

Animal groups

There are two main groups of animals: invertebrates and vertebrates. The invertebrates are a large group of animals that do not have a backbone and skeleton to support their bodies (see chapter 4). Invertebrates include animals with very simple bodies, such as sponges, and more complex animals, such as the insects. The vertebrates are a smaller, but equally diverse, group of animals that have a backbone (see chapter 5). This group includes fish, amphibians, reptiles, birds, and mammals.

Scientists group animals in other ways, too. For instance, invertebrates, fish, amphibians, and reptiles are cold-blooded creatures. Their body temperature is tied to the surroundings, and some, such as reptiles, bask in the sun to warm up. Birds and mammals are warm-blooded animals. They use some of the energy from their food to keep a constant body temperature.

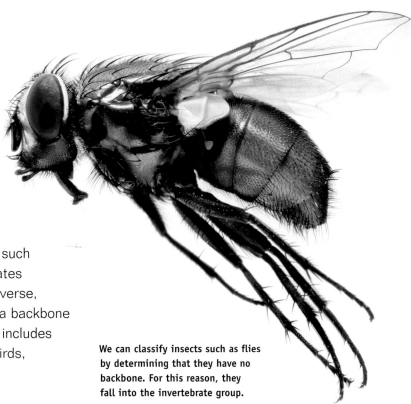

We can classify insects such as flies by determining that they have no backbone. For this reason, they fall into the invertebrate group.

FOOD CHAINS

Every living thing is connected by food chains. Plants are usually the first link in the food chain since they make their own food. Some animals eat plants and form the next link in the chain. The food chain continues as animals eat other animals. Energy passes up the food chain until it reaches a top predator—an animal that is not eaten by any other animal. Microorganisms such as bacteria are another important link in the food chain. They help release the energy locked up in dead animals and plants.

CHAPTER 2

Variation and evolution

No one individual is identical to another member of the same species. Everyone in your class belongs to the same species, Homo sapiens, but you are all very different. Some may have black skin, and others have white skin. Some may be tall, and others are short. These differences between individuals are called variations.

Differences between individuals

Some variations are very subtle. One person might be slightly heavier or taller than another person. Weight and height are examples of continuous variations. Most people lie somewhere in the middle of a range of values. Fewer people are at the extremes, such as heaviest and tallest. Other variations are obvious. For example, you could have blue or brown eyes or you might be a boy or a girl. These are all types of discrete variations, because they can only be one thing or another.

Variations such as skin color and eye color are discrete variations.

Inherited variations

Some features are inherited from your parents. Inherited variations range from eye color to blood group. The instructions for these characteristics are stored in DNA. This molecule is found inside the nucleus of almost every cell in your body. Some DNA comes from your mother and some from your father. If you have a brother or sister, he or she will have inherited a slightly different mix of DNA from each parent.

Environmental variations

Some variations occur naturally during the course of an animal's life. They are called environmental variations. For example, someone who eats a high-calorie or fat-rich diet and does very little exercise will become heavier and more unfit than someone who eats healthily and plays a lot of sports.

Combination variations

Some variations are caused by a combination of inherited and environmental factors. A person

A child who eats a healthy diet and does regular exercise will be thinner than a child who does not. This is an environmental variation.

can inherit the potential to develop a particular trait, but environmental conditions determine whether or not he or she exhibits that trait. For example, a child with tall parents is likely to be taller than most people, but only if he or she has a balanced diet and healthy lifestyle. Other examples of these so-called combination variations include speed, intelligence, and fitness.

INVESTIGATE:
Earlobes

Your earlobes either hang freely, or they are joined to your head. Investigate this example of a discrete variation with your friends or classmates. Make a note of how many people have each earlobe type. Create a pie chart to show what proportion of people have each earlobe type. Is the number with each variation more or less the same in your sample group, or somewhat different? How do you think these results compare with the human population as a whole?

Mutations

Some variations are caused by mutations. When animals grow, one cell divides into two new cells, which divide again to become four cells. When a cell divides in two, it makes a copy of the DNA inside its nucleus. Sometimes mistakes occur in the copying process, and the DNA contains an error. This is called a mutation, and it usually happens by chance. If the DNA contains the instructions for a particular trait, the mutation may lead to a variation.

Natural selection

If a mutation is harmful, an organism is more likely to die out without reproducing. When a mutation is helpful, an animal is better able to remain fit, survive, and pass on the mutation to the next generation. This survival of the fittest is called natural selection.

It is the driving force behind evolution, which is the way new kinds of living things arise as a result of many small changes over time. This idea was first published in 1859 by Charles Darwin (1809–1882) and remains a key theory of modern biology.

New species

Most scientists think that new species appear because of mutations. Consider a mutation in the DNA of some antelopelike animals, which caused their necks to grow slightly longer. As a result, they could feed on the vegetation from taller trees. With little competition for food, the antelopelike animals with longer necks thrived and passed on the variation to the next generation. Slowly, the antelopelike animals with longer necks completely replaced those with shorter necks. A new species formed—the giraffe.

The mutations that resulted in a long neck allows giraffes to feed on leaves high up in trees and so thrive in their environment.

Biodiversity

Evolution is responsible for Earth's biodiversity—the amazing variety of life on our planet. No one knows exactly how many species there are on Earth today— estimates vary from two million to more than 100 million species. Between 5,000 and 10,000 new species are identified every year—most of them are insects found in tropical rain forests.

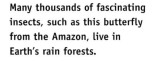
Many thousands of fascinating insects, such as this butterfly from the Amazon, live in Earth's rain forests.

DESIGNER DOGS

Selective breeding of animals such as dogs supports Darwin's theory of evolution by natural selection. More than 14,000 years ago, people domesticated wild dogs. They paired dogs with useful variations to create different breeds, including fast hounds to help them hunt and strong mastiffs to guard their livestock. Recently, people have continued this selective breeding to create many distinctive dog breeds with particular variations in appearance. These range in size from the Chihuahua to the Great Dane.

How to classify

One of the first things scientists do when they classify living things is to tell them apart from nonliving things. A simple way to check if something is alive is to see if it moves. Most animals move to find food and avoid being eaten themselves.

Plants move by growing toward the sunlight, by spreading seeds, and by opening and closing their flowers in response to light, wet, or cold.

Movement alone is not enough to distinguish living from nonliving. Water moves when it flows through river valleys, but this does not mean it is alive. In fact, movement is just one of seven basic life processes that scientists look at when they classify living things. The others are:

- Respiration: the way living things take in oxygen;
- Sensitivity: using senses to respond to changes in the environment;
- Growth: the way organisms get bigger and change as they get older;
- Reproduction: the way organisms produce offspring;
- Excretion: the way organisms get rid of waste products from their bodies;
- Nutrition: using processes to get energy and nutrients from food.

Some of the features scientists use to classify fish include having a body covered with scales and being able to breathe underwater using gills.

STUDYING FOSSILS

Fossils are the remains of ancient animals, plants, and other organisms that are preserved in rocks. Some fossils are leaves or bones. Others are footprints left by animals. The science of studying fossils is called paleontology. Most of the evidence for evolution comes from fossils. They show how much, or how little, living things have changed over time.

Different organisms perform some or all of these life processes in slightly different ways. Scientists group living things based on the similarities and differences in these basic life processes. For instance, birds and mammals breathe in oxygen from the air using organs called lungs, but fish take in oxygen from water using feathery structures called gills. Birds reproduce by laying eggs that hatch into young birds. Human babies develop inside their mother's body before being born.

Looking at the past

Some scientists classify living things by looking at their ancestors. In this type of classification, called cladistics, scientists use computers to compare all kinds of information, such as body measurements, chemical processes, and genetic makeup. Scientists use this information to see how living things are related. They can use this data to develop a "tree of life" to show the relationships between living organisms and identify common ancestors. Recent studies have shown that people and chimpanzees share almost 95 percent of their DNA and are related to a common ancestor that lived around four million years ago.

Although whales swim in the sea as fish do, they breathe through lungs. This is one of the characteristics used to classify them as a mammal.

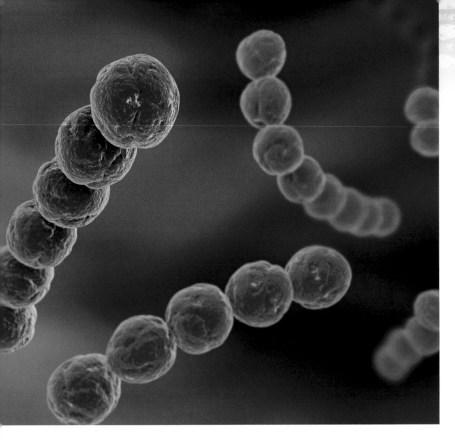

Bacteria, such as these *Streptococcus*, are some of the simplest life forms. They make up one of the five kingdoms of living organisms.

Five kingdoms

Scientists classify the living world in large groups, called kingdoms. They base this classification on similarities and differences in appearance, as well as life processes such as movement, growth, and reproduction. Most scientists agree on a five-kingdom classification, but some think there are as many as eight or more kingdoms.

1. Bacteria

Bacteria are single-celled tiny organisms and by far the most numerous life forms on Earth. They are found in the air, soil, rocks, water, and on or inside other organisms. There are more than 10,000 species of bacteria. Some of them are harmful and cause diseases such as tuberculosis. Others are helpful and help humans by breaking down food within our digestive systems.

2. Protists

Protists are similar to bacteria but have organelles, such as a nucleus, inside their cells. There are around 250,000 species of protists. Some, such as amebas, can move around and feed on other microorganisms. Others, such as diatoms, are like plants and make their own food using the energy from the sun.

3. Fungi

The fungi kingdom comprises more than 100,000 different species, including the familiar mushrooms we eat, as well as yeasts and molds. Fungi are saprophytes, which means they break down the bodies of dead animals and other waste products to feed. Fungi reproduce using tiny structures called spores.

4. Plants

The plant kingdom includes organisms that make their own food using the energy from sunlight (photosynthesis). There are more than 250,000 species of plants, ranging from tiny waterweeds to the giant redwood trees of California.

5. Animals

Animals, such as cats, elephants, and people, are made up of many cells. They get all the energy they need by eating plants or other animals, and they can move around from place to place. Most animals can also sense and react to the world around them using their brain, nerves, and senses. Scientists have identified millions of different animals, but think this represents just a fraction of the total number of species living on our planet.

This tree frog is just one of the 5,000 or more species of frogs that have been identified by scientists. It is likely that thousands more species have not yet been discovered.

GROUPS WITHIN GROUPS

Kingdom is the biggest group in the classification system. Each kingdom is divided into smaller and smaller groups containing species with similar characteristics. In order, these classification groups are:

Kingdom
  Phylum
    Class
      Order
        Family
          Genus
            Species

You can remember the order of the classification groups using this memory aid: "Kings Play Chess On Fat Green Stools."

Biological keys

One way that scientists identify animals is to use a biological key. Biological keys are called keys because they "unlock" information about animals in the same way as a normal key unlocks a door. They do this by asking a series of questions about different animals. By the time scientists have answered all the questions, they should have identified the animals. There are different types of biological keys, including branching keys and numbered keys.

Branching keys

The Greek philosopher Aristotle studied thousands of organisms to find features he could use to classify them. One thing he noticed was that some animals had red blood and some did not. He also saw that some animals had hard bodies and some had soft bodies, and some had shells and some did not. He used these features to group the following animals: birds, fish, insects, jellyfish, lizards, mammals, and shellfish.

The key below is called a branching key because it branches off into smaller groups—just like the branches of a tree split into smaller branches. It is also called a dichotomous key, because each branch splits off into two new branches. (The word *dichotomous* comes from the Greek meaning "divided into two.")

This branching key shows the kinds of differences in characteristics that we can use to classify and group different organisms.

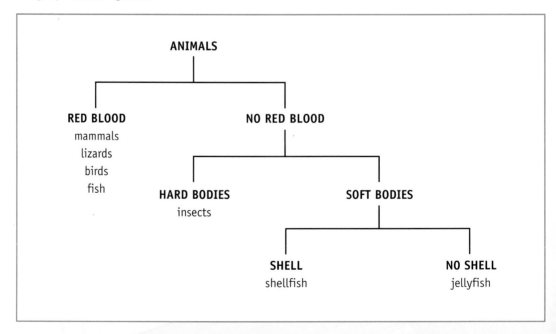

Numbered keys

Some biological keys are numbered keys. In a numbered key, you follow a series of numbered questions by answering "yes" or "no" to each question. Your answer directs you to the next question, until eventually you arrive at the animal you are trying to identify. Use this simple numbered key to identify the animals to the right:

1. Does the animal have an internal skeleton?
   • yes (go to 2)
   • no (go to 3)

2. Does the animal have a pouch?
   • yes (kangaroo)
   • no (horse)

3. Does the animal have six legs?
   • yes (fly)
   • no (spider)

You will use some more biological keys to identify different animals later in this book.

A simple biological key can be constructed to identify four animals: a kangaroo, horse, housefly, and a spider. The key identifies differences in body features, such as how many legs an organism has.

Invertebrates

Invertebrates are animals without backbones. They make up almost 97 percent of all animal species. There are a million or more different invertebrates, and they come in many different shapes and sizes.

Small and large

Most invertebrates are very small, and some, such as water bears, can only be clearly seen under a microscope. At the other end of the scale, the biggest invertebrate in the world is the giant squid. In 2007, fishermen from New Zealand captured a giant squid that weighed an amazing 992 pounds (450 kg) and was over 33 feet (10 m) long.

Supporting role

Since invertebrates do not have a backbone or inner skeleton, they need to support their bodies in other ways. Invertebrates such as worms have fluid-filled cavities inside their bodies. Fluid pressure pushes against the body walls to create a firm core, giving the body its shape and helping it to move. But the cavities can also go floppy, so

WORLD OF WORMS

Almost half of all the invertebrate groups are made up of different worms. These include the peanut worms, which look like peanuts when they contract to their smallest shape; horsehair worms, which resemble dark hairs from a horse's tail; and spiny-headed worms, which grip onto the bodies of sea animals such as seals using the sharp spines on their heads. Worms can shrink or stretch out their bodies to amazing lengths. For example, giant ribbon worms can extend to more than 165 feet (50 meters) in length.

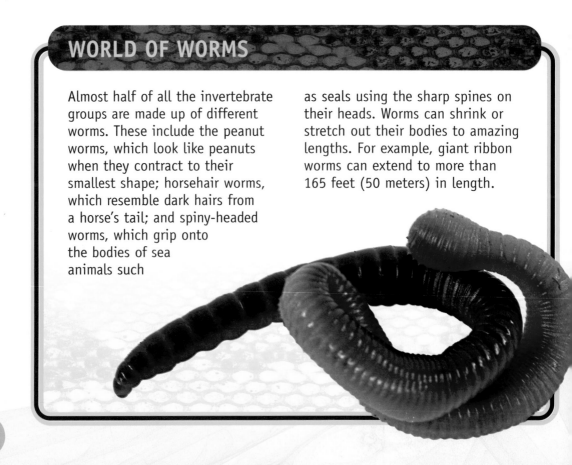

Octopuses use fluid pressure to push their bodies into tiny underwater caves to either hunt for food or hide from predators.

invertebrates can deform their bodies and squeeze through tiny spaces, reach food, or squirt out water to move around. Other invertebrates, such as crabs and insects, have hard outer coverings, called exoskeletons, to support and protect the soft body parts inside.

How to classify

Scientists look at many different body features when they classify invertebrates. One is body symmetry. Many invertebrates, such as flatworms and snails, have what is called bilateral symmetry. This means you could draw an imaginary line down the center of their bodies—from end to end—and the two halves would be mirror images of each other. Other invertebrates have what is called radial symmetry. This means that similar body parts, such as tentacles, are arranged evenly around a central point. Scientists also look at other things to make a classification, such as the position of mouth, number of body parts, and whether body parts are continuous or divided into segments.

Sponges

Sponges have the simplest body structures of all animals. Most of these simple invertebrates live in the oceans, especially in tropical waters, although a few are found in fresh water. They spend most of their lives attached to rocks or other underwater surfaces.

There are about 10,000 different sponges, and they come in many shapes and forms. Most consist of an outer layer of tissue covered with a regular pattern of small holes. Water flows through these holes into channels that lead to a fibrous inner layer. Cells in walls of the sponge have tail-like parts that drive water through the channels and filter out tiny particles of food. The nutrients from this food are shared by all the cells in the sponge.

Sea anemones, corals, and jellyfish

Sea anemones, corals, and jellyfish form another group of simple marine invertebrates with hollow bodies and an opening for a mouth. For instance, jellyfish are bell-shaped, floating tubes with stinging tentacles hanging down around a central mouth. All of these invertebrates are armed with stinging cells. The cells shoot out microscopic stinging barbs, similar to tiny harpoons. In anemones and jellyfish, the barbs can stun and kill animals and the tentacles draw in the prey to eat it. Sea anemones have fleshy, tube-shaped trunks, and their stinging cells are on the upward pointing tentacles that fringe their mouth. Coral barbs stick to prey so the coral can digest them.

Scientists have identified more than 1,500 jellyfish species. They are found in all the world's oceans, and a few species are also found in fresh water.

BUILDING A CORAL REEF

Coral reefs are the biggest natural structures made by any animal. They start to form when free-swimming coral larvae attach themselves to underwater rocks to form a coral polyp. Each polyp uses calcium in seawater to build a hard case of limestone. The limestone case has a hole at the top through which the polyp's tentacles can poke out. Millions of polyps form a continuous structure that we call a coral reef.

Coral reefs form mainly in the shallow, warm waters along tropical coasts, where plenty of sunlight can penetrate the water. Microscopic plants called algae live inside the bodies of the polyps, and the algae need sunlight to make food by photosynthesis. The coral polyps benefit from this relationship because they take some of the food made by the algae.

Coral reefs teem with life. A complex food chain exists within the reef: the plants that grow on the reef provide food for fish and other organisms, which in turn are eaten by larger creatures such as sharks.

Worms and leeches

Worms and leeches are simple invertebrates with bilateral symmetry. The group includes segmented worms, roundworms, and flatworms. They are all relatively small and have long, soft bodies with no legs. They move by contracting muscles in their bodies, which forces fluid to different parts of their bodies. In this way, they can stretch out their heads, shrink back into spaces, and wriggle along.

Earthworms and the blood-sucking leeches are segmented worms. As their name suggests, the bodies of these worms are divided into segments. The earthworm has tiny bristles on either side of each segment, which it uses to anchor against soil and pull its body through underground burrows. Roundworms are generally transparent and too small to see. Some roundworms, such as ragworms, have tentacles around their mouths to sense their surroundings. Some live freely, most notably in the soil. Others are parasites that live inside, and get their nutrients from, other animals. Flatworms have flat, thin bodies. Unlike other worms, they do not have an anus and excrete waste through the mouth. To find food, some flatworms have simple eyes on their head. Many are also parasites, including tapeworms and liver flukes.

The lines on this leech's body show how it is divided into segments.

Five-sided

Starfish, sea urchins, brittle stars, sea lilies, and sea cucumbers belong to a group of around 7,000 invertebrates that live on the sea floor. All of them have bodies with five sides, which is known as "radial symmetry." They have a spiny exoskeleton just under their skin that can be rigid, as it is in sea urchins, or flexible, as it is in starfish.

A sea urchin's body is covered with sharp spines that deliver a poisonous sting if touched.

The most striking feature of these marine invertebrates is the water vascular system. This system works like a hydraulic pump. Water-filled tubes spread through their bodies, and their muscles force fluid through them to move the arms or spines. Starfish have five or more arms with tiny tube feet on the lower surface. When the tip of a tube foot touches a surface, water is withdrawn by the water vascular system, creating a suction effect. This helps the starfish cling to rocks on the sea floor. Some starfish use fluid pressure to push their stomach through their mouths, to engulf their prey and digest it without actually eating it.

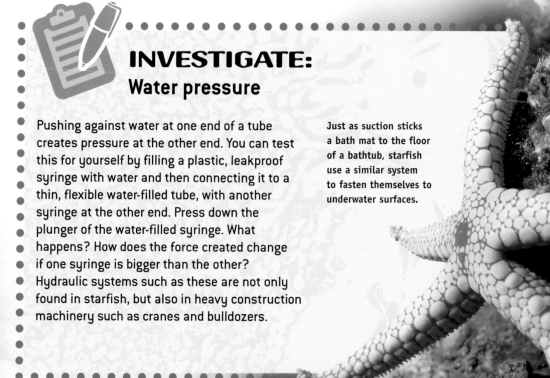

INVESTIGATE:
Water pressure

Pushing against water at one end of a tube creates pressure at the other end. You can test this for yourself by filling a plastic, leakproof syringe with water and then connecting it to a thin, flexible water-filled tube, with another syringe at the other end. Press down the plunger of the water-filled syringe. What happens? How does the force created change if one syringe is bigger than the other? Hydraulic systems such as these are not only found in starfish, but also in heavy construction machinery such as cranes and bulldozers.

Just as suction sticks a bath mat to the floor of a bathtub, starfish use a similar system to fasten themselves to underwater surfaces.

In a shell

With more than 70,000 species, mollusks are the second-biggest group of invertebrates. The word *molluskus* means "soft-bodied," so most mollusks are encased in one or two shells for

The jagged line on this oyster shell marks where its two hinged halves meet.

protection. The soft body consists of three parts: the head, the main body mass, and the muscular "foot," which the mollusk uses to move. Some mollusks, such as snails and whelks, have a single spiral-shaped shell, which can also take a more symmetrical form, as in cowries. Other mollusks, such as mussels, oysters and scallops, have two shells that meet at a hinge. These mollusks are always found in water.

Feeding and moving

Some mollusks, such as snails, feed using a radula, which is a ribbonlike tongue covered with sharp ridges. They use their radulas to scrape food from the surfaces of rocks.

LOST SHELLS

Slugs are mollusks just like snails, but they have no obvious shell. In fact, some slugs do have a very short visible shell, and most have shell granules under their skin. This adaptation helps slugs burrow through soil, sand, and dead leaves. Land slugs produce large amounts of slime to protect them from drying out. Sea slugs often have bright colors to warn predators that their slime is poisonous.

Other mollusks feed by filtering particles of food from the water. The food gets trapped as water passes through the mollusk's gills when they breathe. Mollusks such as snails glide along on a film of mucus secreted by their foot. Others move by forcing water out from their shells or bodies, or by stretching their feet to grip surfaces before pulling the rest of their bodies along.

Heads and tentacles

The biggest group of mollusks are the cuttlefish, octopuses, and squid. These marine invertebrates have large heads and brains in relation to the size of their bodies, which consist of a muscular tube, usually without any shell. Cuttlefish, octopuses, and squid move by jet propulsion! They suck in water through a siphon tube and squirt it back out of their bodies to escape from predators.

The long, oval-shaped section of a cuttlefish is its body. The animal's huge eyes are found on either side of its head, which also contains a sharp beak for tearing up food.

Some species have highly developed sense organs. For example, an octopus uses its large eyes to detect the shape, size, brightness, and position of objects, although it cannot see in color. The muscular "foot" of an octopus is modified into eight muscular tentacles. The octopus uses them to crawl around, capture prey, and transport food to its mouth. Squid also have two long tentacles that can shoot outward to suck onto prey. Cuttlefish, octopuses, and squid have a radula like snails. They also have a tough beak at the center of their ring of tentacles. They use the beak to break up prey into small pieces.

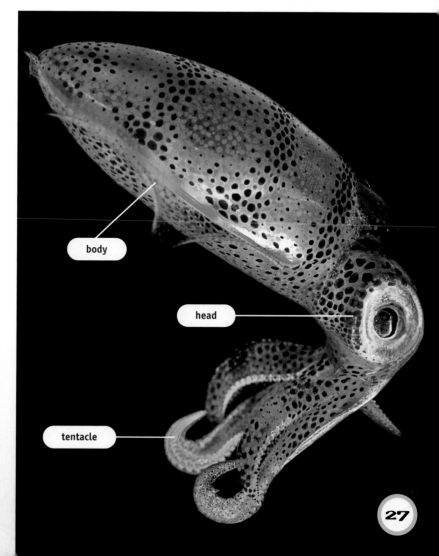

body

head

tentacle

Armored invertebrates

The arthropods are the largest group in the animal kingdom. Around half of all known species on Earth are arthropods. No one knows for sure how many species there are, because most have not been discovered. The figure could be as high as 10 million. Although there is enormous variety within the group, all arthropods share certain features. They have segmented bodies covered by a rigid exoskeleton—body armor made of a tough substance called chitin. They all have jointed legs, too, so they can bend their limbs to swim, crawl, jump, and run.

An extremely powerful and poisonous sting is delivered by the tail of a scorpion.

Spiders and scorpions

There are four main groups of arthropods. The first includes spiders and scorpions. These invertebrates have two body segments, four pairs of legs, and a pair of jointed mouthparts. Spiders and scorpions often use venom to kill prey, which they inject using fangs, or in the case of scorpions, the sting at the end of the tail.

Centipedes and millipedes

The second group includes centipedes and millipedes. These invertebrates are known for their many legs—some millipedes have more than 370 pairs. Centipedes have one pair of legs on each body segment, and millipedes have two. Centipedes move quickly and hunt prey using venomous claws. Millipedes are slower, more rounded in cross section, and eat plants.

Crustaceans

The third group is the crustaceans, which includes crabs, shrimps, lobsters, wood lice, and barnacles. Crustaceans have very hard exoskeletons. Their bodies are divided into three segments—the head, thorax, and abdomen.

Crustaceans have four pairs of walking legs attached to the thorax. Barnacles are unusual crustaceans because they stick their shells on rocks on the shoreline. When the tide comes in, they open the shell and use their legs to filter food from the water.

Insects

Insects are by far the biggest group of arthropods. All insects have three body segments—head, thorax, and abdomen—and three pairs of legs attached to the thorax. Wingless insects, such as springtails, are the simplest insects. Among the winged insects, some lay eggs that hatch into miniature versions of the adults. Insects of this group include termites, grasshoppers, and walking sticks. Other winged insects lay eggs that hatch into maggotlike larvae, which undergo a dramatic change, called metamorphosis, to become an adult. These include bees, butterflies, and beetles.

The exoskeleton of a shrimp protects the soft flesh of the body inside.

INVESTIGATE:
Invertebrates

Can you identify the following invertebrates using the biological key below?

A

B

C

D

1. How many legs does the animal have?
   6   Go to 2
   8   SPIDER
2. Does the animal have wings?
   YES   Go to 3
   NO   ANT

3. How many wing pairs does the animal have?
   1 pair   HOUSE FLY
   2 pairs DRAGONFLY

Vertebrates

CHAPTER 5

Vertebrates are animals with backbones and an inner skeleton made of bone or cartilage. There are about 50,000 vertebrate species—just a tiny fraction of the total number of species living on Earth. The main groups are fish, amphibians, reptiles, birds, and mammals.

Support and protect

Strong bones support a vertebrate's body, and this has allowed some species to grow to huge sizes. The elephant is the largest animal on the land, and the blue whale is the largest animal that has ever lived.

The vertebrate's skeleton protects the organs inside the body, most notably the brain inside the skull and the heart and lungs within the rib cage.

A vertebrate's bones are connected at joints and are moved by muscles, allowing a huge range of movement. Indeed, the vertebrates are some of the fastest animals on land, in the sea, and in the air.

The elephant is the largest animal that lives on the land. A typical elephant will be more than 10 feet (3 m) tall and weigh several tons.

Sensing the world

All vertebrates have a well-developed central nervous system. The major nerve is the spinal cord, which runs through the center of the backbone. The spinal cord connects the brain to the rest of the body through a vast network of nerves. The nerve network also connects the brain to the sense organs, which include eyes, nose, tongue, and sensory whiskers. These sense organs are on the head, close to the brain, so that information can pass from the sense organs to the brain very quickly.

A fish's movements are controlled by the messages sent from its brain along its backbone to its body.

How to classify

Some of the questions scientists ask when classifying the vertebrates relate to life processes and include:

• Do they lay eggs or give birth to live young?

• Is their skin covered with scales, feathers, or hair?
• What are their bones made of and how are they arranged?
• Do they breathe in oxygen from the air, or do they live underwater and breathe in another way?

Can you think of some examples of vertebrates that fall into these groups?

INVESTIGATE:
Vertebrates

The five main groups of vertebrates can be identified using this dichotomous, or branching, key. They are amphibians, birds, fish, mammals, and reptiles. Can you identify the missing three?

ALL VERTEBRATES

Has hair: Has no hair

Has feathers: Has no feathers

Uses gills: Uses lungs

Has smooth skin: amphibian   Has scales: reptile

Fish

Fish are the main group of vertebrates found in watery habitats such as rivers, lakes, and the ocean. They are cold-blooded creatures and breathe by taking in oxygen from the water using feathery structures called gills. They all have sleek, streamlined bodies and fins to help them cut through the water as they swim. Most species are covered with scales, and they reproduce by laying soft eggs.

The flat body of a ray is supported by cartilage, the same material that is found in a human's nose!

Fish groups

The main way scientists classify fish is by looking for similarities in their skeletons. Eels, goldfish, and trout belong to a group called the bony fish. Members of this group have skeletons made of hard bone. Their teeth are also partly made up of bone, which fixes them into the upper jaw. Sharks, skates, and rays belong to a group called the cartilaginous fish. The skeletons of these fish are made of a tough, flexible cartilage, similar to the rubbery tissue that makes up our ears. Cartilaginous fish do not have bony teeth; instead, they have sharp scales for teeth.

Sharks, skates, and rays

Bony fish and cartilaginous fish share the main features of all fish, but there are also many differences. There are around 1,000 different species of sharks, skates, and rays. All of them have mouths underneath their snouts and

between five and seven gill slits along each side of their bodies. Their scales are pointed, making their skin very rough to touch. Cartilaginous fish have a very acute sense of smell. They also have sensitive pits on their heads to detect the electricity generated by other animals as they swim.

Sharks have powerful tails, which are usually longer at the top than at the bottom. This shape helps sharks swim fast as they hunt, by pushing their bodies up in the water. Sharks swim with their mouths open. Swimming pushes water through the mouth and past the gills so they can breathe. Skates and rays have flat bodies with winglike side fins. This body shape is perfect for life on the sea floor.

Bony fish

The bony fish are by far the biggest group of vertebrates. There are around 29,000 species, ranging from the small sticklebacks and guppies, to the enormous marlin and porcupine fish. Bony fish differ from cartilaginous fish in many ways. Bony fish can breathe without swimming. They gulp in water and close their mouths, which forces the water out past the gills. A hard plate, called an operculum, covers the gills.

Bony fish are powerful swimmers, too. They have smooth, overlapping scales to cut down on drag. They also have a swim bladder, which they fill and empty with air to help them float and sink.

Sardines are the young of fast-swimming bony fish called pilchards—a common food fish for people.

WITHOUT JAWS

A small and unusual group of fish are the jawless hagfish and lampreys (below). These fish have circular mouths edged with sharp teeth.

Many use their mouths like suckers, clamping down on the bodies of other animals to feed on their blood and flesh. Jawless fish do not have scales or paired fins, and they only have a single nostril on top of their head. The ancestors of these fish were probably some of the first vertebrates to appear in the oceans.

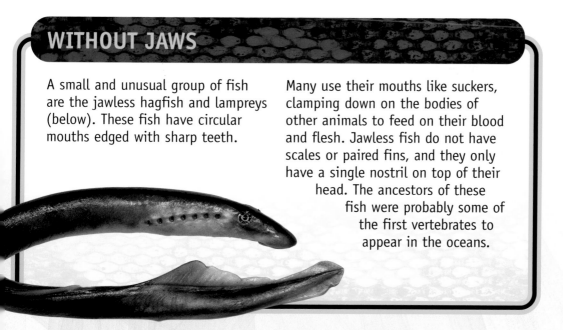

Amphibians

Amphibians are cold-blooded vertebrates. Most spend their adult lives on land, but return to the streams and ponds to breed and lay eggs. The eggs usually hatch as larvae that take in oxygen from the water through gills. The larvae then slowly change through metamorphosis into adults with lungs to breathe in air. Many adult amphibians can also breathe through their thin scaleless skin. Glands in the skin produce slime to keep the skin moist out of the water. Some species secrete chemicals through their skin that taste bad and deter predators. Others, such as the poison dart frog, produce poisons that are powerful enough to kill people. These amphibians have bright colors as a warning that they are dangerous.

Different groups

There are two main amphibian groups: frogs and toads, and the newts and salamanders. Frogs and toads make up 90 percent of all amphibian species. Adult frogs and toads have large heads but lack tails, and the back legs are longer than the front legs. Toads differ from frogs by having more even-length legs, warty skin, and short tongues.

This tree frog has large eyes and a wide mouth with a long, sticky tongue to catch prey, such as insects, in the rain forest.

WORMS WITH TEETH?

The third amphibian group is the caecilians. There are around 175 species, some 3 feet (1 meter) long. Many lack legs and eyes and resemble large worms. Caecilians live in Asia and South America. They burrow through soil or the muddy riverbed in search of worms and other prey, which they grasp with their teeth.

Newts and salamanders look a little like lizards. A typical newt or salamander has a long body that ends with a long tail. These amphibians can have four or sometimes just two similar-sized legs. Some species have crestlike fins along the top of their backs and tails.

Double life

The word amphibian comes from Greek words meaning "double life," which reflects the differences between adults and larvae of many species. The larvae of frogs and toads are called tadpoles. They are very different from the adults and look remarkably like small fish with long tails. But not all amphibians hatch as larvae—young salamanders look like mini versions of adults. And not all amphibians lay their eggs in water— some tree frogs lay eggs in a special foam they make from their slime.

Salamanders have weak, splayed legs that can barely lift their bodies off the ground as they move slowly along.

Reptiles

Reptiles are vertebrates with dry, scaly skin. Their scales are hard and protect the reptiles" soft insides. The scales also prevent them from losing water through their skin. Reptile eggs have soft, leathery shells. Unlike fish and amphibians, they lay their eggs on land. Even reptiles that live in water, such as sea turtles, return to land to lay their eggs. All reptiles have lungs, not gills, so those that live in water have to surface to breathe air.

Reptile groups

There are four main groups of reptiles. More than 95 percent of reptile species are snakes and lizards. This group of reptiles has skin covered with horny scales. Most species have long bodies and tails; lizards usually have four legs, but snakes have none.

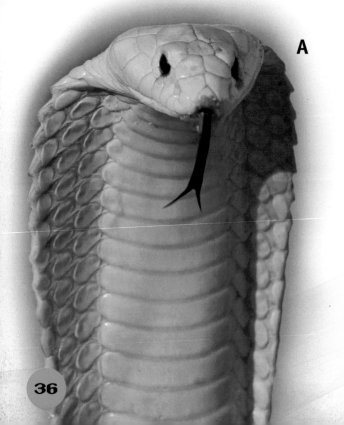

A

There are 23 species in the group of crocodiles and alligators. These large reptiles look a little like lizards but have heavily armored skin and long, toothed jaws with at least 60 teeth.

Tortoises and turtles are a group of reptiles with domed shells called carapaces. The carapace is an extension of the reptile's backbone and consists of a leathery skin (in the case of turtles) or horny plates (tortoises).

Two ancient, lizardlike creatures, called tuataras, make up the fourth and final group of reptiles.

Reptile variations

Reptiles come in many different shapes and sizes. Lizards called chameleons have turret-shaped eyes that can move independently. The chameleon's specially jointed toes help it grip branches as it hunts for prey, which it snaps up with a long, sticky tongue. Lizards called geckos are unusual because they have no scales on their heads. Geckos have special skin under their toes that helps them climb up surfaces as smooth as glass. Snakes such as boas and pythons kill their prey by coiling their bodies around the body of their victim and slowly squeezing it to death. On the other hand, cobras and vipers use fangs to inject a deadly venom to kill their prey.

B

C

INVESTIGATE:
Reptiles

Can you identify the reptiles on these pages using the numbered key below?

1. Does the reptile have legs?
   YES   Go to 2
   NO   SNAKE

2. Does the reptile have a hard shell?
   YES   TURTLE
   NO   Go to 3

3. Does the reptile have overlapping scales?
   YES   LIZARD
   NO   ALLIGATOR

D

Birds

There are 29 main groups of birds, which include about 9,000 different species. Perching birds, such as crows, sparrows, and starlings, make up more than half of all these species. The feet of these birds are adapted to perching, with three toes pointing forward and one pointing backward. Perching birds are often known as songbirds, because many species, such as nightingales, have distinctive calls. Other bird groups show a wide range of variation. Waterbirds such as ducks and seagulls have webbed feet to help them swim. Pelicans have four webbed toes and often large, bare throats that expand to hold fish. Parrots have powerful curved beaks and thick tongues for breaking seeds and other hard plant parts. And owls and other birds of prey have large, forward-facing eyes for spotting prey from a distance.

What makes a bird?

Birds have beaks in front of their skulls. The beak contains no teeth but has heavy jaws. All birds have wings, which are modified front legs. Almost all birds use their wings to fly. Feathers cover the body. The biggest feathers are on the wings. These "flight" feathers are wide, light, and push a lot of air out of the way as birds flap their wings.

Birds are light for their size to help them stay in the air. They have air sacs connected to their lungs. The sacs store air that refills the lungs as birds breathe out. As a result, birds can take in much more oxygen from the air, which makes flying more efficient. Bird bones are light and spaces inside the bones fill with air from the air sacs, too. A few birds cannot fly. Ostriches have tiny wings compared to the size of their bodies, and so they cannot generate enough lift.

Birds of prey, such as this peregrine falcon, hover high up in the air to spot prey and then swoop down to catch it with their sharp talons.

Penguins use their curved, stiff wings as paddles to swim through the water at high speeds. Some species can reach speeds of 9 miles per hour (15 kph) in pursuit of prey or when escaping predators such as leopard seals.

NEW LIFE

Birds lay eggs with hard shells. The parents sit on the eggs or bury them to keep them warm, so the young inside can develop properly. When they are ready to hatch, the chicks use a small projection called an egg tooth to break out of the shell. The parents of most species care for their young. They feed the hatchlings for days or weeks after hatching. Some, such as gulls, regurgitate or bring up partly digested food from their stomachs. Flamingos and pigeons go one step further by feeding their young on high-fat, high-protein "milk" produced in the bird's stomach.

A young spoonbill reaches into its parent's beak to take the food it regurgitates.

Mammals

There are about 4,500 mammal species on Earth, ranging in size from the huge blue whale to the tiny bumblebee bat. Humans are mammals, too. All mammals share several features. They are the only animals with hair, or fur, on their bodies. Mammals are the only animals that sweat to cool down. Female mammals feed their young with milk from their mammary glands.

Reproduction

Scientists have identified three main groups of mammals based on the way they reproduce.

Placental mammals such as humans develop inside their mother's womb, so they are highly developed at birth. A placenta supplies nutrients to the developing baby as it grows inside the womb.

Marsupials such as kangaroos develop inside their mother's womb, but only for a few weeks. The young are poorly developed at birth, so they crawl into a pouch in which they can suckle milk and grow further.

Monotremes are unusual egg-laying mammals. There are two monotremes: the duckbill platypus and the spiny anteater (echidna). The young hatch from eggs and feed on milk that oozes from their mother's mammary glands.

Mammal food

One of the main ways to tell different mammals apart is by looking at their teeth and how they eat. Rodents such as beavers, mice, and squirrels make up the largest group of mammals. They have large, curved incisors shaped like chisels for gnawing tough food. Carnivores, such as cats and seals,

Spiny anteaters are monotremes. As their name suggests, these animals use their long nose to dig ants from their homes and then eat them.

A kangaroo's baby is called a joey. Even when the joey is strong enough to survive on its own, it may still hop inside its mother's pouch if it is frightened.

have sharp canine teeth to puncture and kill prey. They have tough, ridged carnassial teeth to chew flesh and bones. Some mammals have no teeth. Humpback whales have hairlike fringes hanging from their jaws that filter food from water like a net.

Getting around

Scientists also tell mammals apart by the number of their toes or how they move. Bats are the only true flying mammals. They have long, narrow fingers with stretched skin between them to form wings. Whales have no back legs but a wide, horizontal tail. The whale's thick front limbs act like paddles to help it swim. The ungulates are a group of mammals with hooves. Hoofed mammals may be odd-toed or even-toed. Odd-toed ungulates include horses and rhinos. Even-toed ungulates include camels and pigs.

CLOSE RELATIONS

The closest relatives to humans belong to a group of mammals called primates. This group includes the marmosets, monkeys, and apes such as the chimpanzees (right). Primates have large brains in relation to their body size, so they are intelligent. They have forward-facing eyes, and most have opposable thumbs, which means the thumbs bend toward the fingers. This allows the primates to grip and manipulate small objects. Humans are the only primates that always walk on two legs.

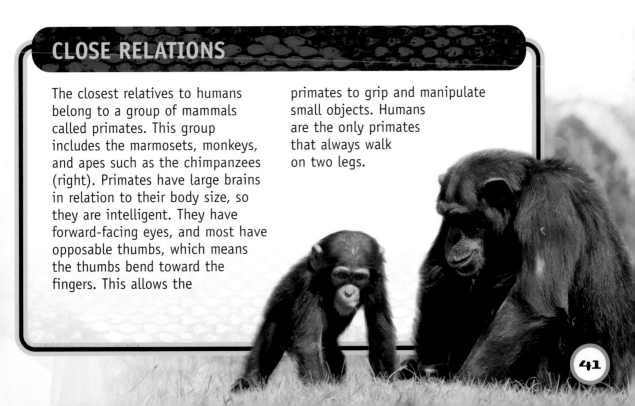

Classifying common birds

In this activity, you will create your own classification key to identify some common birds. First, you will make some bird feed to put out in your yard, school grounds, or local park. Then you will spend some time watching the birds as they feed. You can use a field guide to birds to identify the different species, or if you have a camera, you could take some pictures and look up the bird species on the Internet. Then you will ask some questions about the birds to identify similarities and differences between them, which can be used to compile a classification key.

Making the bird feed

The first thing you need to do is to make some bird feed.

You will need:

- string
- scissors
- yogurt tubs
- butter
- mixing bowl
- bird seed (available from pet shops)
- peanuts
- breadcrumbs, pieces of fruit, and other kitchen scraps

1. Cut a few pieces of string. Use the scissors to pierce a hole in each yogurt tub. Thread the string through the hole and tie a knot. Pull the string tight up to the hole.

2. On low heat, melt the butter in a microwave. Be careful when melting butter—it can get very hot. You may need to ask an adult to help you.

3. Pour the liquid butter into the mixing bowl and add the bird seed, peanuts, and kitchen scraps. Stir the mixture, taking care not to splash the fat.

4. Spoon the bird feed mixture into the yogurt tubs and press it down. Allow it to cool in the refrigerator.

5. When the butter has cooled, slide the yogurt tub off the bird feed mixture. You can now start the next part of the activity.

Hanging the feeder

Now you need to hang your bird feeder in a suitable place. You could run a clothes line between two trees and hang the feeder from the line. This will keep the feeder away from tree trunks, fences, and anything else that predators, such as cats, can climb on. It will also deter animals such as squirrels, who will try to eat the bird food.

Bird watch

Set aside half an hour every day for a week to watch the feeder—maybe in the morning before you go to school. Make sure you are hidden to avoid disturbing the birds as they feed. Then take photographs or draw pictures of the birds. Look at a bird spotter's guide or the Internet to identify them.

Constructing the key

When you have identified the birds, start to construct your classification key. Look at the similarities and differences between the birds. For example, you could sort the birds by size into small and large.

At the top of a piece of paper, write down the question "Is the bird large?" Draw two arrows leading away from the question, one marked "Yes" and one marked "No." Then look for another feature that can be used for identification, such as type of bill (see box) or color. Each question will help you divide the birds into two groups, until eventually you are left with only one bird in each group. Stick your drawing or photograph of the bird below the final question in the key.

To check your key, go back to the beginning and pick a bird at random. Follow the questions through the key. If it works, you should end up at the bird you have chosen. If not, you will need to check the questions you have asked.

Ask a friend to identify a bird in your key to double-check that it works.

BILL PROFILE

The main job of a bird's beak or bill is to help it to feed. Its shape varies according to what the bird eats. As a result, you can use bill shape as one of the features to identify the birds at your feeder. The table below shows you some of the beak shapes and how these relate to what the birds eat:

The cracker bill
Birds such as finches and sparrows have short, thick bills to crack open seeds.

The tweezer bill
Birds such as titmice have short, pointed beaks to snap up small insects, seeds, and nuts.

The probing bill
Thrushes and blackbirds have long, thin beaks to probe inside snail shells and pick berries.

The multipurpose bill
Crows and other general feeders have a multipurpose bill to eat a wide variety of foods, such as seeds, fruit, and insects.

Glossary

abdomen The end section of an insect's body.

adaptation Characteristic that helps an organism to survive in its surroundings, and cope with its diet and lifestyle.

algae Plantlike organisms that do not have leaves, stems, roots, or flowers, but make food by photosynthesis.

antennae Sense organs found on the head of some animals, such as insects and crabs.

camouflage Hiding by blending in with the surroundings.

cartilage Tough, flexible tissue that supports the body of some animals.

cell The basic building block of all living organisms.

central nervous system The brain and spinal cord—the control center of an animal's body.

class Classification group that contains one or more orders.

cold-blooded Term used to describe animals that cannot control their own body temperature.

colony Community of organisms.

continuous variation Variation between individuals in which the differences can take a range of values.

discrete variation Variations between individuals in which the differences are either one thing or another.

DNA Deoxyribonucleic acid, the chemical from which genes are made.

embryo Organism in its early stages of growth.

evolution Process by which every living thing slowly changes over time because of the slight variations in genes from one generation to the next.

exoskeleton Hard, protective body covering of animals such as insects and crabs.

family Classification grouping that contains one or more genera.

fungi Plantlike organisms that do not contain chlorophyll and so cannot make their own food. Mushrooms, molds, and yeasts are fungi.

gene Sequence of DNA that carries one piece of genetic information.

genus Classification grouping that contains one or more species.

gills Feathery structures used by some animals to breathe underwater.

habitat Place where an organism lives. There are many different habitats in the world, ranging from mountaintops to the ocean depths.

invertebrates Animals that do not have backbones.

larva Stage of growth of some organisms after hatching from an egg, different in form from the adult. Insect larvae are wingless and resemble a grub.

metamorphosis Complete change of physical form from a larva (such as a tadpole) into an adult (such as a frog).

mutation Change in DNA affecting an organism's characteristics.

natural selection Process by which organisms best adapted to their environment tend to outlive and take over from those that are less well-adapted.

nerve Bundle of fibers containing nerve cells.

nucleus Structure inside a cell that contains genetic information.

nutrients Substances that organisms need to live.

order Classification grouping that contains one or more families.

organelle One of a number of different structures found inside cells. The nucleus is an organelle.

organism Any living thing, such as an animal, plant, bacterium, protist, or fungus.

parasite Organism that lives on or inside another organism.

photosynthesis Process by which green plants trap energy from sunlight and use it to make food from carbon dioxide and water.

phylum Classification grouping that contains one or more classes.

placenta Organ that nourishes young mammals inside their mother's womb during pregnancy.

predator Animal that hunts other animals for food.

prey Animal hunted for food.

pupa Stage of growth when a larva metamorphoses into an adult.

respiration Process by which organisms release energy from food using oxygen.

scales Overlapping or interlocking bony plates that form a protective layer over the skin of reptiles and fish.

species Basic classification grouping. Male and female individuals within a species can mate and produce fertile offspring.

spore Reproductive unit of some plants and fungi.

thorax Middle section of an insect's body that bears wings and legs.

vertebrates Animals that have backbones.

warm-blooded Animals that can maintain their body temperature using the energy from their food.

womb Part of a female mammal's body where an embryo develops (also called the uterus).

Further information

BOOKS

Animal Kingdom Classification series by Steve Parker and Daniel Gilpin (Compass Point Books, 2005)

Variation and Classification by Ann Fullick (Raintree, 2005)

WEB SITES

Due to the changing nature of Internet links, Rosen Publishing has developed an online list of Web Sites related to the subject of this book. This site is regularly updated. Please use this link to access this list: http://www.rosenlinks.com/lpr/anvar

Index